Abortion and the Ransom of the Sacred

Damian P. Fedoryka

Christendom Press

To His Holiness
Pope John Paul II

The Philosopher who by Divine Providence
Became the Pope of Human Dignity
Because he first
Became the Pope of Divine Sovereignty

In Grateful Appreciation
These Reflections are Dedicated

. . . for by its very condition human nature is subject to God in a threefold manner, First, according to the degree of goodness . . . Second, human nature is subject to God by virtue of God's power. Third, human nature is subject to God in a special way by its own proper act: in as much, namely, as it obeys His commandments by its own free will. And this threefold subjection to God Christ confessed of Himself.

. . . This third subjection He also attributed to Himself saying, according to John 8:29, "Whatever pleases Him I always do." And this is the submission of obedience. Because of this Paul says in Phil. 2:8 that He was obedient to the Father even unto death.

— *St. Thomas Aquinas*

Foreword

Those who perform, or who support the performance of abortions, have succeeded at this time in the great struggle over abortion in the United States in framing the public debate largely in terms of the unborn child as a "thing" and the present legal freedom to procure abortions as a "right" enjoyed by every woman. The success of the abortionists and their supporters has come only after two decades of propaganda which began with the constantly repeated claim that the unborn child was nothing more than a mass of tissue living, parasite-like, in a woman's body. In successive stages, as science demonstrated the falsity of that claim, the humanity and then the person of the child has been denied.

Now, in the post-Cruzan and Dr. Kevorkian era, arguments which seek to defend the unborn child by demonstrating its life, humanity and personhood all seem to be futile in view of the mind-set, which is becoming increasingly common in the United States, which holds that human life is a *thing* which one can appropriate and dispose of for whatever reason seems "good" to oneself.

It is to challenge this radical mind-set that Dr. Damian Fedoryka has written this brilliant essay. Following the lead of the phenomenologist philosopher, Karol Wojtyla, and his later writings as Pope, Dr. Fedoryka has, with great clarity shown the absurdity, and the ultimate danger, of the trend towards valuing human life solely in terms of its utility or worth to other individuals or to society as a whole. The consequences of the Cuomo-Kennedy syndrome, "I am personally opposed, but . . ." is shown which has already been responsible for such a toll in human life.

All of us engaged in the struggle to save the lives of unborn children, comatose patients and the elderly and disabled are indebted to Dr. Fedoryka for this significant contribution to the respect for human life debate.

Rene H. Gracida
Bishop of Corpus Christi

Table of Contents

I. Abortion: The Forgotten Dimension of Justice

In a number of his talks and exhortations, especially to academic audiences, Pope John Paul II speaks of the need for a deeper understanding of the human person. This essay is a response to the Pope's challenge for a deeper concept of the human person. It takes as its basis the Pope's own frequent references to *man's capacity to give himself* as an essential mark of his humanity and dignity.

The Pope has a remarkable sense for the spirit and mentality of the age. He distinguishes the legitimate aspirations of man from the dynamic attractions which mislead him and threaten the loss of his dignity. Thus, he affirms man's freedom and power of self-determination as one of the grounds for his dignity as a human person. At the same time he recognizes the legitimate desire that contemporary man has for participating in those decisions that determine his destiny as an individual, as a member of a family and of the larger economic and political groups.

In the context of contemporary man's "search for himself," the Pope teaches and warns that man can truly find himself only when he "makes of himself a sincere gift" to others and ultimately to God Himself. Thus the basic condition for self-discovery and true self-actualization is the act of self-donation, of giving oneself to another. In former times and cultures, one would have spoken of devotion, loyalty, commitment, fidelity and sacrifice. The basic word for this gesture, as Karol Wojtyla, the priest, said in one of his sermons, is *"Thine."*

If the act of self-donation realizes man's vocation, it presupposes a specifically personal capacity, that is the capacity or power to possess one's being. For nothing can be truly given unless it first belongs to the giver. Thus the ability to utter "Mine" effectively is a precondition for meaningfully saying "Thine."

Perhaps the single most decisive feature of the modern age is contemporary man's determination to utter the basic word "Mine" without proceeding to complete it with an act of self-donation and commitment to another person. The central and all determining category of our era is that of appropriation and self-appropriation. It is embodied in what Pope John Paul II refers to as consumerism.

"Mine am I, so that I can be Thine." This is the response called for in man's dialogical situation. Yet, modern man cuts short the dialogue with the affirmation

"Mine I am so that I can be. . . !" Man's existence has been reduced to the act of appropriation. "Being is having!" All being, the whole of creation is appropriated in the gesture of incorporation. It is consumed so as to become merely a part of and extension of man. The sovereign gesture of appropriation creates a kingdom without a king, for the man who utters "Mine" becomes himself consumed, a slave to the inner need and its demand for satisfaction.

As a priest, Karol Wojtyla reflected in his sermon on "Fatherhood" on the importance of learning to be like a child as the condition for fatherhood. The basic word of the child is "Thine." As creatures, we must all learn "Thine," the language of self-donation to God the Father.

After reflection, it becomes relatively easy to see that with the unconditional "mine" and the loss of the capacity to say "Thine" comes a loss of the sense of what constitutes a gift and especially a loss of the understanding that the *very existence of every human being is a gift*. In receiving the gift we depend on the donor. And in receiving the gift we recognize that the donor gives himself in the gift. So, in recognizing the gift character of our life, we recognize that God gives Himself, that he becomes Father as well as Creator in giving the gift of life. And we become children as well as creatures of God. But in refusing to acknowledge that we belong to God, we fail to take possession of our being, however much one may insist that his life is unconditionally "his."

As a philosopher, the future Pope elaborated the notion of self-possession as central in the understanding of the human person. This notion that the person is *sui juris*, that he or she belongs to himself, retains a decisive place in the teachings of Pope John Paul II. But it is always "completed," as it were, by the notion of self-donation, which becomes the dominant theme.

The formal concepts of "self-possession" and "self-donation" are relatively new in Catholic theoretical thought. Nevertheless, the reality they talk about is nothing new. They capture, in different language, the basic alternative and warning voiced by Christ Himself, "He who seeks to save his life will lose it; he who loses his life for my sake, will find it." They do have the peculiar feature, however, of helping us focus with greater theoretical clarity on this basic alternative. In the hands of John Paul II they do contribute to that greater understanding of the human person which he frequently calls for.

The present essay focuses on the problem of abortion in terms of these notions of self-possession and self-donation. The stress on the facts that human life belongs to God, that it is a gift to man, that man is called to take it "into his own hands" and that he must do so in order to fulfill his creaturely vocation of giving himself to God allow us to see more clearly that in abortion we are dealing with the "taking possession of the life of another" and with a *grave injustice*.

The sharpening of recent debates about abortion as well as the increase of tensions in social and political life show unmistakably that the abortion debate is couched for the most part in terms of *morality* and *immorality*. One of the most frequently heard phrases on the side of the proponents of abortion is one to the effect that one ought not impose one's morality on others. Thus, many politicians, even Catholics, insist on the separation of "personal morality" from "public policy."

As a consequence, we notice the tendency to stress dialogue, debate and persuasion. The very suggestion that legislation, and hence force and sanctions be brought to bear on the abortion issue is interpreted as a violation of rights and a coercion. This position is persuasive for many precisely because it contains a grain of truth in it.

Moral acts (as distinct from external behavior) consist of voluntary and free internal acts. In this they resemble religious acts which are also voluntary and free internal acts. The Second Vatican Council says clearly in its *Declaration of Religious Liberty* (#3) that "acts of this kind cannot be commanded or forbidden by any merely human authority."

If one wanted to sabotage the prolife movement one could do so by taking a series of small and simple steps.

First, identify the prohibition against abortion as a matter of morality or religion.

Second, invoke the letter (the spirit can't be invoked here) of the Second Vatican Council and its declaration on religious freedom: "acts of this kind cannot be commanded or forbidden by any merely human authority."

Third, one is now in a position to separate "personal morality" from "public policy" which one proceeds to do as expeditiously and righteously as possible. This allows one, of course, to maintain the air of personal integrity ("I personally would never do something as dastardly and horrible as. . . .") as well as public probity ("I would never betray my trust as a public servant and allow my personal morality to influence the performance of my duties of defending the right to. . . .")

We can now understand the persuasiveness of Senator Kennedy in his criticism of the American Bishops. Their expressed position was that it was logically untenable to separate personal morality from public policy. Senator Kennedy, for his part, as reported by the *New York Times* of September 10, 1984, told us that this cannot mean that every "moral command" must be sanctioned by law.

Today it has become a commonplace that "personal morality" should be separated from "public policy." This commonplace figures as one of the criticisms of the

American Bishops' expressed intention of hiring a public relations firm to help them mount a national campaign against abortion. The Catholic Church is welcome to express its moral and religious teachings, goes the objection, but how dare it try to make these a matter of "public policy?"

The answer is very simple, of course. If abortion is a matter of personal immorality, which it decidedly is, it is so primarily because it is *first* a matter of injustice toward *another* human being. Kennedy was right if the Bishops wanted to make a logical connection between personal morality and public policy. For no such logical connection is apparent. How does one get from the idea of personal morality — the sphere of inner acts — to public policy, that is, to public actions?

But *abortion is already public*. It takes the life of another human person. The facts that this other person is in the womb, or that its life is taken in the privacy of an operating room or clinic, or even that the woman makes this decision "privately," none of these make the taking of another's life a private matter. *And abortion is unjust* because it takes the life of an innocent human being. Hence, because it is public and unjust it must become outlawed as a matter of public policy. Nothing is more obvious than the fact that here we are not legislating morality or religion; rather, we are legislating justice.

It is significant that the Catholic Church, whose primary and direct concern is the inner moral condition of the soul and its salvation, seems to suspend this concern when she speaks about the injustice and crime of abortion. In the former matter, she has the power of the keys. In the latter matter she has no power and can only exhort, teach and persuade. Yet she always speaks of abortion as an injustice. When she proclaims in *Gaudium et Spes*, #51, "Life must be protected with the utmost care from the moment of conception: abortion and infanticide are abominable crimes," she is speaking in defense of the innocent victim, and not addressing herself to the immorality of the agent.

On September 18, 1984 Pope John Paul clearly identified abortion as an "unspeakable crime against human life." He was proposing nothing new, but simply repeating what Vatican II said in its *Gaudium et Spes*. In section 27, murder, genocide and abortion are listed as crimes along with other violations of human dignity, such as:

> subhuman living conditions, arbitrary imprisonment, deportation, slavery, prostitution, the selling of women and children, degrading working conditions where men are treated as mere tools for profit rather than as free and responsible persons...

Again, in the context of the above passage, there is no question of immorality. To be sure, all behavior that produces the above crimes is also immoral. But in the above context the Church is speaking against their injustice and in defense of human dignity and rights. The Church does not possess the power of the sword which it can wield in defense of the innocent, but, as the Sacred Congregation of the Faith notes in its *Declaration on Abortion*, "the Church cannot remain silent on this question." Its defense of the rights of men is for the most part limited to teaching and persuasion. And she does, as always, teach. In that same document she addresses herself to the frequently invoked freedom of thought, and says that it may never be invoked as "justification for attacking the rights of others, especially the right to life." In that same document she goes on as follows about this right:

> The right to life is the primordial right of the human person. The person has other goods, some of them even more precious to him than life, but the right to life is the foundation and condition for all others. It is not within the competence of society or public authority, whatever its form, to give the right to some and take it away from others. Any such discrimination on grounds of race or sex, skin color or religion, is *always unjust*. The right to life does not derive from the favor of other human beings but exists prior to any such favor and must therefore be acknowledged as such. The denial of this is an *injustice in the strict sense of the word*.

On December 9, 1972, Pope Paul VI, recalling Vatican II, reminded us that the responsibility of defending the right to life has been entrusted to men. It is not the Church that has the power or mission to do this. On the contrary, "it is a mission which rests on every human being, every intermediary community (starting with the family) and, above all, on the political community."

Manifestly, the mission of defending the right to life cannot be restricted to a defense in the form of teaching and persuasion. Defense here implies the proverbial "sword," that is, the use of power or force that has public effectiveness. This is primarily and by priority the task of civil authority. In *Casti Connubii* we are reminded of the perennial teaching of the Church in this matter:

> Those who hold the reins of government should not forget that it is the duty of public authority by appropriate laws and sanctions to defend the lives of the innocent, and this all the more so since those whose lives are endangered and assailed cannot defend themselves.

Here again, the focus is not on the immorality of the perpetrators but on injustice and the helplessness of the innocent victims. It is imperative, if the defense of innocent human beings is to be effective in both debate and action, that we *focus on the moment of justice rather than morality when dealing with abortion in the public sphere*. In what follows I make the attempt to do so by following the lead of John Paul II by resorting to the overriding importance of self-possession. In doing this, I follow what has been implicit in the teachings of the Church all along, and what has also been made explicit in the *Declaration on Abortion*, which says the following about man and society:

> He lives his life in close connection with his fellows, and is, as it were, nourished by reciprocal personal communion with them amid an intimate coexistence in society. Over against society and other men, *every human being has the right to possess himself, his life* and the various things that contribute to it; all others have a *strict obligation in justice to respect that right*.

It is my judgment that a discussion of abortion in terms of the fundamental character of human self-possession will allow us not only to gain a deeper understanding of the human person but also to reorient debate as well as action into a more effective defense of the innocent, who, precisely in virtue of their innocence, can claim that we belong to them as much as we belong to ourselves.

II. Abortion: Keeping God in the Picture

The ire of the abortionists rises at the least suggestion that abortion *ought not* be permitted. "That's religion," they object, "how dare you violate my rights by imposing your opinions on me. Keep God out of it." Similar objections and slogans were presented by homosexual activists during the demonstrations that attended the desecration of St. Patrick's Cathedral and Our Eucharistic Lord.

Some of us are indeed tempted to leave religion, or at least the Catholic Church, out of it. Many of us may in fact feel uneasy about imposing religious opinions, if not Catholic teachings, on others. Faced with the stricture to keep our religion to ourselves, our minds may hesitate and balk even as we dig our heels in.

But look at the matter a bit more closely. Why should we leave God out of it when it is the murderer himself that drags God into it? Why should we cringe at the notion of imposing our opinions on others when it is the murderer himself that imposes a terrible burden on us?

Homicide, very simply, is the *taking* of a human life; murder is the *deliberate taking* of an *innocent* human life. The Catholic Church has always taught that the intentional and unjust taking of human life is unconditionally wrong. It is something that *never* ought to be done. She is clear and unwavering in this teaching, even as she recognized the legitimacy of *preserving* and defending my life against unjust aggression. Human life has ultimate importance. That is why, in defending myself I am only allowed to use the least force necessary. Very simply, I am not allowed to use a bomb if a firecracker will stop the aggressor. And I am not allowed to *intend* killing the aggressor. I can only intend to stop the aggressive action. In other words, I ought not *want* the death of the aggressor. And finally, so great is the importance and dignity of human life, that I am not allowed to use the death of another person as a *means* to an end, however great and noble. When I use the death of another person as a means, I do want his death. And that is wrong.

In taking a human life, the abortionists perform what is essentially a *divine* action. They act as if they were God, and then ask us to respect this sovereign act.

With the claim to a divine prerogative, it is the abortionist that brings God into the picture. Whatever, the claims that religion and God are a private matter, murder makes the action public. It challenges not only God but also us.

For we are now burdened with the *obligation* of responding to the innocent human being's cry for help. The abortionist commits murder for the sake of an education, or health, for the sake of freedom from care or even for a few extra dollars at the end of the month. Because of his or her action we are now called to risk *our* education, our health, our comfort and material resources, indeed, even our lives for the sake of the innocent life being taken. All of this is imposed on us by the murderer.

The problem is that many of us, even those adamantly opposed to murder, do not always realize just what the *taking* of human life is. The full reality of it seems to get lost behind commonplace words. We take an aspirin, we take a nap, we take a walk. Nothing dramatic here. We can do without that word. Substitutes can serve: we swallow an aspirin, we nap, we go for a walk. We say exactly the same thing; only in different words.

But then, we "take a life!" Even the abortionists sense that we have to do with murder. They try verbal substitutes: "The right to choose," "Reproductive freedom." They no longer say the same thing. They hide behind abstractions. Very well, we speak of an abstraction, the right to choose. But the right to choose what? Or of the right to one's body. But how about the body of the innocent person being murdered? Not ignorance, but the cold blooded intent to ignore reality is enshrined into law. In this instance circumlocution, "speaking around" the subject without naming it, is a sign of cowardice. Only rarely do we find the courage of the one who is clear about the issue and speaks of abortion as the taking of a human life even as one claims a *right* to abortion.

Some are courageous enough, — audacious is perhaps the proper word, — to admit that abortion is the taking of human life. They draw their audacity from the claim that a woman, and consequently her abortionist, have a *right* to take human life. What does this mean? And in answering, let us by all means not be "judgmental" lest we make dialogue a bit too difficult for the abortionist. When I "take" a human life, I "appropriate" it; I lay hands on it as if it were my own, as if it belonged to me. Now, someone, perhaps even the one whose life is being taken, may raise an objection. Imagine me walking into your house and appropriating your living room couch, or laying my hands on your television, or taking your wallet. "Hey, wait just a minute! That's mine. How dare you walk into *my* house and just take *my* things? Get out of here or I'll call the police." We don't have to be writers to imagine the dialogue.

In ancient times the *sacred* had a special status. Sacred was what *belonged* to and was reserved to "another." And more specifically, something was sacred because it belonged to the gods. One dared not enter into or appropriate the sacred without permission of the gods. Indeed, even then, one had to be purified, in other words, to become worthy.

It is imperative that in any discussion of abortion we keep in mind the fact that human life is sacred, namely that it belongs to God. This means that no one, not even we, are allowed to "take possession" of our own lives and being without permission. Our own lives are sacred not only with respect to an aggressor who would take it, but also with respect to ourselves. This means that no woman, or man for that matter, can legitimately say that his or her life or body is absolutely his or her own! The abortion proponent's claim that it is the woman's body defends just such a claim to absolute possession of both the woman's body and that of the child about to be aborted. But it is precisely that claim that brings God into the picture. We must force the issue precisely by challenging the claim of the abortionist. On what basis can he or she say that anything, much less their bodies, is their own?

III. Abortion: Claiming Human Life and Death, or the Politics of Appropriation

So, where are we? You come into my home and claim my living room couch, my television and even my wallet. I threaten you with the police for daring to take what is mine. Two competing claims. Each saying "mine." Which one is true, that is, which claim is *valid*? We are asking in other words, who has the right? Now, a right is not merely a claim. Anyone can make a claim. Anyone can reach out and try to take possession of something. The real question is whether the claim is justified or valid, in other words, is it a right? When does something truly belong to me in such a way that I can truly call it my own and reject external claims to it?

The matter isn't too difficult in the case of my home and my possessions. Under normal circumstances the police would protect me, almost by reflex. Apparently the police have lost that natural reflex when it comes to abortion.

So, we return to our dialogue with the abortionists. We see, and they acknowledge, that they are taking a life, claiming it as their own. They say they have a right to take it. My simple question is: How does it happen that this life belongs to you? How do you justify your claim?

Notice what happens. The woman claiming the child's life usually says, "my life, my career, my body, my health." I don't dispute for the moment that all these things are hers. The interesting thing is that she also claims that the child is hers. We won't dispute that either, for the moment. The truly astounding thing is that because the woman would be rid of the child(!), the abortionist claims it as his own, and takes it. Now it is the abortionist that says "mine" of that child. Nay, it is not astounding, it is simply incomprehensible. How can it be that because one person, the mother, discards and rejects a child, another person, the abortionist, somehow suddenly acquires possession of a child and a right to take its life? If I throw out my living room couch, my television or even my wallet, then surely the principle of "finders, keepers" would apply.

But a child is not a thing. A child is a person. It can neither be discarded with impunity, nor can it simply be appropriated. The reason for this is that no human person can say "mine" of himself in the full and radical sense. Much less can he legitimately say "mine" in this way of another human person. And this because he is a created, contingent person.

How, then, and in what sense, can we say "mine" of our own being, if we can say it at all?

A person can have or acquire title to something in different ways. First, it can be the *author*. When I create or produce something it is mine. My ownership is justified by and grounded in my authorship. Second, I can acquire title to something by virtue of it being a *gift* to me. And third, I can gain title simply by claiming and taking possession of something that does not belong to anyone else. In this instance it is simply my *power* to hold it that establishes my ownership.

But there is a fourth, a mysterious but real way in which something can become "mine." Something can be mine in virtue of an *obligation*. Every parent, especially the contemporary parent, is in a position to recognize this, particularly when the young child, perhaps in an exaggerated gesture of independence, says, "You don't own me, it's my life, it's my money, I can do with them as I want." The proper response should be, "As long as you are *my obligation* you will obey me!"

Things, especially people, enter into the orbit of what is *ours* when we are bound by an obligation in their regard. By virtue of the fact that I am obligated to take responsibility for something or someone, I become *bound* to it.

But the moment I say this, and reflect on it, it suddenly strikes me that there is still another, a fifth way in which "belonging" can occur. Because of my obligation to the child, for example, the child can claim me as belonging to it. Because of that obligation not only does the child belong to me, I belong to the child. The child can say of me, with full justification, "Mine!" Indeed, it seems that children have a greater claim to say "Mine" about the parent than the parent can say "Mine" of the child. This changes, of course, as the parent grows old and helpless.

The helplessness of another human being, his need becomes the basis for an obligation and binds me to him in a unique and special way. We have in mind here not his helplessness with regard to a luxury, his lack of those things that make life comfortable. Here certainly it is not self-evident that we are bound to provide them. What we have in mind are those goods and benefits without which life or human dignity would be at risk. Because we are bound to do him good, the needy human being has a claim on us. We become his in a fundamentally real way. And we can no longer invoke what is "ours" and deny it to him.

Every one of us, especially the parents, belong to the unborn child, whose most basic good and benefit, that is his life, depends on us. It is nothing less than a dissonance of cosmic proportions when a parent who belongs to the needy child invokes the "mine" as a justification for taking the life of the child.

When the parents turn against the unborn child, we, all of us, come to belong to the child, even if in different measures. All of us, in our helplessness as creatures, have a certain legitimate claim on God with respect to the true goods and benefits of our existence. Even though we are creatures, we can nevertheless make so bold as to say "Our . . ."

"Hold it!" I hear the proponent of abortion objecting, "I know what you're leading up to. You're trying to bring God into it again. You can't fool me. 'Author,' 'creator,' . . . that's religious nonsense and totally unscientific. I don't believe in God, so don't try imposing your beliefs on me!"

Very well, let's not impose God on our abortionists. The question remains, nevertheless. How did they acquire ownership of their being? If God is not the author and creator of their being, perhaps their parents created or produced them. If that is the case then they belong to the parents. But our abortionists could hardly support such a primitive line of thought. It would tangle them up in the very thing they are trying to avoid. For if they belong to the parents who "produced" or "created" them, then the only way they could come into possession of their own selves is either by emancipation or by revolution. The parents either set them free, the way a slave owner would emancipate a slave or they would, by sheer will and power, break the bonds of ownership by rebelling. We can see that the curious logic of the pro-abortionist would lead him to choose the rebellion of children against their parents as the way of acquiring freedom. For emancipation of children by parents or slaves by owners would imply being given a gift of one's own freedom and therefore of one's own being. But if it is a gift that can only be hoped for but never claimed, title to my being can be given to third parties.

We can see the complications. Not the least of which is that children could not have abortions without the permission of parents. Saying that the child belongs to the parents is apparently too high a price to pay for justifying an abortion. Much better to promote rebellion of children from the parents or even better, to dispossess the parents of the children by an act of the state. But this too poses a problem. Ownership by the state, though preferable to ownership by parents, is no more palatable. The proponents of abortion clearly have a problem. They cannot allow that title to one's own being originate in the authorship of parents or in the parents' donation of a gift. The only solution is to *affirm power* as the grounds for the title to one's own being.

But to claim something by virtue of power is a divine act, in form if not in substance. It remains an imitation of God, as it were, when exercised upon minerals and vegetables, perhaps even upon animals. But when power is not only the justification but also the very stuff of taking possession of another created person, it becomes an *anti-theistic* act. For in claiming the life of another as his own, the contingent creature rises up to challenge God, Who alone owns human life.

It would be tempting to say that the proponents of abortion treat unborn children as things and not persons; that they have forgotten what it means to be a person rather than a thing. It may be so in some instances. Unfortunately the matter is deeper and more complex than that. The consistent and persistent abortionists grasp accurately the radical alternatives: either human life belongs to God, the creator and source of human life, or it belongs to no one and "comes to nothing."

Their rejection of God's legitimate claim to human life forces them, with an iron clad logic, into the negation of life. They cannot be "pro life." They are necessarily "pro death."

IV. Abortion: The Theft of the Sacred, or the Politics of Power

God is the author and creator of the contingent person. This is not a question of "revelation" or "religion" but a basic fact given to those who possess the use of reason. My parents are "pro-creators" of the biological and psychic components of my being, but my personal center, my soul is produced neither by my parents nor by my body. It is by virtue of this free personal center that I can possess my self and determine myself in performing *free acts*. That is what we mean when we say man is a *person*.

The individual untouched by the corruption of the contemporary technological ethos, the "primitive" man we might say, has a profound experience of facing some sovereign power whenever he encounters in nature a being that exists and acts according to *its* laws. He grasps intuitively that such a being does *not* belong to him even as he is *allowed* to take possession of it and to use it. But here too he realizes that when he uses what belongs to another, he must "pay the price" to gain title to it.

The primitive had a keen sense of the fact that he was surrounded by the *sacred*, that is, by something that belonged to another who stood above other men. He was surrounded by a kingdom of which he was not the king, a kingdom which he could enter only with permission and only at the price of recognizing the sovereign.

How much, how infinitely greater is the sense of a sovereign sphere and center when we encounter another person! We are faced with a being whose actions and behavior come forth from a free center in his being. Cats and dogs behave the way they do because they are determined by their nature. They can't help behaving the way they do. We could say that they are slaves to their nature. The person, however, is called to be the master of his being. *He* and not his nature determines whether he will lie or tell the truth, whether he'll be faithful or faithless, whether he helps another or turns in upon himself. He and his free acts belong to him infinitely more than his body or his external possessions. Here too the sphere of the *sacred* shows itself, but in a much more pronounced fashion.

Our abortionist may object that we are products of evolution and not creatures of God. The theory of evolution gives many an atheist the security of what he takes to be a rational refuge against the ravings of the "mystics." Why invoke God when we have a perfectly rational and scientific way of explaining how we got here? But in his satisfaction he suspends the use of the very reason he invokes. For if he stopped and thought just for a moment he would realize that nothing, produced by man can pick itself up and do its own thing. Every human product is strictly bound by the laws of nature and the structures imposed on it by man. And remember, man, the *rational animal*, planned, calculated, measured, engineered, experimented, used his vast intelligence but could produce something that behaved only the way that he, the producer, determined. Nothing produced by man has or will be able to make *its own decisions*. Nevertheless, our rationalist is trying to say that the blind and dumb laws of nature could produce something that one day would "break away," as it were, claim its own being, and say "my being, my body, my life," and then even more amazingly, *"my decision"* and then proceed to act on it.

But even more mind boggling is the claim that the whole chain of evolution, whose every link is *self-centered* and existing *for itself*, could, after eons of activity, produce a species the individuals of which could give up their lives *for the sake of another!* The evolutionist is confounded by this possibility. In all his clear headed rationality he must ignore the ultimate measure and the ultimate possibility of human existence: "Greater love hath no man than to lay down his life for his friends!" He must blind himself to the implications by saying that this is some animal instinct striving "for the preservation of the species." He has to deny that man could by a *free decision* give up his life for the sake of another person. He has to reduce it to some blind instinctual legacy of evolution. And yet, he himself claims to rise above natural law, to be free of the instincts of nature in order to behave rationally and make his own decision: but always for his own sake and benefit, never for the sake of another.

How ironic that the proponents of abortion propose to destroy in another the very thing that they invoke. "It is *my* decision, *my* choice!" They claim ownership of their own being in order to justify destroying the life of another . . . and bring us back to the issue: Just how does one acquire "ownership" of one's being?

If the abortionists reject God as the creator and source of the life which is given us as a *gift*, they are left only with *power*. The modern, scientific and civilized pro-abortionists grasp, rather feebly, at blind and irrational power as their explanation. But mere power does not justify. You may indeed be strong enough to take possession my living room couch, my television, my wallet and even my life. But your appropriation is wrong and *unjust*.

Have we come to a dead end? It would rather seem so, in one sense. No further dialogue is possible.

Confronted with a radical and intransigent "I will" which neither offers nor accepts reasons for or against, we can no longer reason, argue or debate. In another sense, however, this impasse is in effect the death verdict for the abortion position. It provides us with a new beginning if only we realize all the implications.

At a very minimum we must understand that for the abortionist it is a matter of power and only power. We can no longer waste time and energy trying to reason with the abortionist. It would be an irrationality of sorts, wouldn't it, trying to reason when no reasons are admitted. No, the primary task is to show the abortionist not that he should not or ought not, but that *he will not take another human life* because we will prevent him from doing it. We must proceed as we would with all other mindless threats to life: use power or flee. But since it is the life of an innocent other that is at stake, we cannot flee.

A second point: we are *obligated* to use power. We not only have a reason for using it, we also have an obligation. In the face of the value and innocence of the victims which *bind* us to help them we cannot invoke freedom, or the fact that it is my life, my body, my fortune which is claimed by the victim. We cannot, in other words, use the "arguments" of the abortionists. To say that we can only discuss, debate, dialogue, in one word, that we are only allowed to try changing the *opinion* of the abortionists is to do the very thing that they are doing: it is to ignore the *right* to life of the victim.

As I mentioned before, one of the ways in which another person comes to "belong" to us is through our obligation in his regard. We become in a real sense *bound* by the widows, the orphans, the poor, the helpless and defenseless. But to that extent we belong to them. Confronted by their need, we no longer "belong to ourselves." Here we recognize a distinct source of community rejected by the abortionist. The helplessness of another, especially of the victim of aggression, creates a legitimate claim on those of us who are in a position to help. The right to life of the victim not only obliges the aggressor to desist, but also obliges us to defend the victim. The right to life addresses itself to us as much as it binds the aggressor.

Once again we return to the issue. The right to life is grounded in the fact that an individual has a *legitimate claim to possess his own being*. While he can give himself or his life to or for another, no other can legitimately take it. We can recognize the *fact* that a person has the *power* to possess his being. We see this in every free act in which the person makes a free decision. But what is it that justifies and makes this power legitimate? What explains the fact? We must go beyond the mere fact of the power, otherwise we have no case against the abortionist.   Without grounding this power in something other than itself we have no argument against either tyrant or aggressor. Indeed, there would be no such thing as unjust aggression.

We have been given our being by God, the author of our lives. And we have been given our being so that we can return it to God in an act of devotion and self-donation. Nothing can be given unless it belongs to the giver. Thus, we have been given the *power of self-possession* so that we can give ourselves to God and to other persons. This means that we can belong to ourselves only because in a more fundamental and basic fashion we belong to God. We belong to him as do all creatures. But we are also called to belong to him as *persons*, namely as giving ourselves freely to Him. But this also means that we are not to take possession of the being of another person.

"There you go again! You've done it again, you brought God into it! You are trying to impose your faith on me." So we have. And we are not. But we will stop you!

V. The Public Role of God and the Cuomo-Kennedy Principle

We are not trying to impose our faith on the abortionists but are only trying to give them a chance to understand several things. First, there is a reason, indeed, a sufficient reason, for action to stop them from murdering innocent children. Second, the very fact that their, as well as our, lives belong to God is the reason why we will not use our power arbitrarily against the abortionist. And third, if the last thing shook them back into sensibility, we must affirm that God does not need some special title to enter into our temporal sphere, life and activities.

It is a modern fiction that God is a "private" matter and that the life of men in public cannot be bound by the reality of God if there be even but one who rejects God. To the extent that this fiction prevails in public life, man cannot be considered as even belonging to himself — unless he has the power. And nothing would preclude one from taking possession of another, unless it be the greater power of the other, of the group he belongs to, or of the state. Cynics have claimed that God is an invention of the weak precisely as a last resort against the strong. But the cynic is blinded by his own cynicism. The strong would have to be very stupid or very infantile to be thwarted by an imaginary power. What the cynic doesn't understand is that it is God's *justice*, not his power, that is a bulwark against unjust use of power.

The cynic takes God to be an imaginary being because he does not see the power of God intervening to save the widows, the orphans, the poor and defenseless. But he is also blind to the fact that the taking of another life is unjustified precisely because it belongs to God Who gave it to each individual. God may not intervene with His power, but it is God that *justifies* the use of power by men in the defense of other men against aggression and exploitation. And this in several ways.

First, on the most basic level we are bound to protect everything that belongs to Him. It is because of God's *sovereignty* that even a complete stranger has a legitimate claim on us for help. All superior, that is, truly humane cultures recognized this. The stranger, the traveller, the guest were under the protection of the gods. The fact that we have a common Creator and Master is the most fundamental basis for the community of man.

Second, human existence is a *gift* to the individual. This implies, as I have tried to show elsewhere, that *God gives Himself in the very act of creating a human person*. It is a specific form of sacrilege, therefore, to take another human life. It constitutes a specific form of defiance of God and a frustration of His self-donation to a created person. The direct taking of a human life is not only directed against man but also against God. It is anti-theistic. By virtue of the above, the taking of a human life is an injustice against God. Here I am bound by the other not by the fact we belong to the same Lord and Master, but because the other is the *object* of a loving self-donation on the part of God.

Third, the personal, loving God wills that the created person give himself to God in adoration and love. In and through the act of *submission*, the created person can belong to God in a new and unique sense. God's sovereignty and lordship is manifested in a supremely higher fashion when the created person submits and gives himself freely to God. Self-donation as a power belongs necessarily to the essence of personhood. And it presupposes the power of self-possession. Man is his own, he has been given ownership of his being so that he can give himself. The taking of human life therefore also includes a further distinct injustice against God. It deprives Him of a *subject* in the full sense of the word. In the case of abortion it makes impossible even the beginning of a self-donation to God.

But abortion is *also* an injustice against the victim. His being, from the first moment of existence, is reserved for him. The call to possess himself so that he can give himself to another constitutes an absolute barrier and prohibition for other creatures. His being is in this sense sacred. In taking a human life the abortionist appropriates what belongs to another by right, and thus commits a grave injustice against him.

The grave injustice against the victim is a direct source of obligation to others to come to his defense. When unjustly attacked, the claim that he has on his life extends out, as it were, not only to the aggressor but also to all those in a position, that is, those who have the power to help him. This claim is sanctioned, or confirmed by God. We are now obliged to take responsibility for the life of the victim. He now belongs to us in a unique fashion and we to him. But we are also responsible to God for the life of the victim who depends on our help as a condition for keeping his life.

At this point we encounter something as interesting as it is significant: the claim of the victim extends to those men who are in a position to respond to that claim. We are on the horizontal level. The claim originates from man and is addressed to man. The question arises, does God claim or demand of us that we protect or come to the aid of a victim? Is there a claim that descends from God to us in the vertical dimension? If, as we said, man belongs to God, then God also can say "Mine" of the victim over against the aggressor. How does He do it? Obviously He can do it by direct revelation. But, as far as I know, there are no aggressors who bear testimony that God intervened asking them to desist.

God's sovereignty over what is His own is represented by what we call *public or civil authority*. Thus, in addition to the victim's horizontal claim to our help we *also* have God's vertical claim on us to defend and protect what belongs to Him. It is God's sovereignty that is the basis for legitimate civil authority . . .

"Oh my goodness. I can't believe it! Theocracy! You are trying to establish a theocracy . . . in this day and. . . .," the pro-abortionists register their objection. Not a few evangelizing enthusiasts have become completely unnerved at the charge of being theocrats. But we must not be deterred and remain faithful at least to the gods of dialogue. Let us therefore assume for a moment that God's sovereignty does not extend into the civil order. What remains can best be explained by illustrating the Cuomo-Kennedy principle, the other alternative. This principle, for those who don't know it, states that a public official must suspend his personal views and opinions about a subject and enforce the law, no matter how odious the actions protected by the law.

The Kitty Genovese incident, which occurred in 1964, is well within the memory range of the older generation. The young woman was slowly and brutally murdered in the streets of the Bronx as she desperately screamed for help within sight and hearing of at least thirty eight witnesses. Not one of these made the least gesture even to summon help.

One way of explaining civil authority is to say that we, the people, elect someone to represent us, authorizing him to act on our behalf. Thus, a community of, let us say, thirty eight people, upon seeing someone unjustly attacked, would, on this account, elect someone, a Cuomo or a Kennedy, to act on their behalf. By accepting the election, the representative would have to suspend his personal interests (or at least that used to be the theory) and serve his constituency. On this account also, the elected representative would have to act to save the victim, while the rest of us could sit back, at least until the next election. Thus, he might personally favor the aggression against Kitty Genovese but would have to bracket his personal opinions and act on behalf of his constituency which wills to save the victim. So far this sounds good. As long as the "people" has the *will* to defend the innocent. But what happens when the "people" doesn't want to, or even positively wills not to defend the victim? What if a Cuomo or a Kennedy were elected to represent those who positively wanted Kitty Genovese's murder to occur? At that point the elected representative would have to say, "While I'm personally opposed to attacking Kitty Genovese, as a public servant, I have to enforce the law, that is, the will of the people to defend anyone who wants to attack a young woman in the streets."

Kitty Genovese's claim to help is a justified one, even if the law of some state were to give males a "right" to attack young women on the streets of any city. So is the claim of the unborn to be helped and defended an objective claim, regardless of any actual law on the books. In terms of our previous discussion, it is a claim on the horizontal dimension, the dimension which exists between men. In each instance the legitimate claim binds each one of us *individually*. But even if all the individuals decide to choose a representative to act on their behalf, they do not create a *public or civil authority*. They may authorize the one to act on behalf of all of them. Yet this authority can never stand *above* the individuals. It has its source in the individuals and derives from them. If they take that authority away, the representative loses it. In that case they would still be individually obligated to come to the help of Kitty Genovese or the child threatened by abortion. They are still bound by the "authority" of the victim who demands, in justice, to be defended.

The Cuomo-Kennedy principle appears to be valid only on the assumption that civil authority has its origin in the collective will of a plurality of individuals. On that account we would never have any basis for objecting to the murder or oppression of any minority, if that should happen to be the will of the majority. We might "personally" favor and work for a change (if the majority allowed it, that is) but would have no basis for saying that such oppression is unjust.

In fact, public or civil authority finds its legitimacy from *above*, that is, in the *vertical* dimension that exists between God and man. Public authority does not represent the interest or the will of the individuals composing a society. Indeed, public authority does not even represent the interests of the victim as such. That is why the individual who exercises public authority must give up, as it were, his personal interests and even beliefs. His authority must, in that sense, be exercised in an impersonal fashion.

Legitimate public authority represents the interests and sovereignty of God. It reflects the fact that every individual human life belongs to God. In that sense it is the public presence of God in the affairs of men and in human society. The representative of a collective venture has to answer to the group. God does not have to answer to any collective. Human existence is His venture and project. The collective venture may call for sacrifices, but the collective can never sacrifice a single human individual for the benefit of the collective. None of this would hold if man did not belong to God. But because he belongs to God, not even the defense, by legitimate authority, of the victim of an injustice is justified simply by the interests of the victim. We may quite confidently say that continued life might be too great a burden, that it would bring with it suffering and misery, the victim himself, if consulted, might express the wish to die, yet we are not justified in *taking* his life, because that life belongs to God.

The same reasons, discussed at the beginning of this section, which justify the intervention of *individuals* in the defense of human life also justify the action of a *public authority*, indeed, even to a greater extent. For it can never be said that it is just the interest of an individual or a collective that binds and obligates men.

VI. Separation of Church and State, or "One Issue" Politics

The historians can sort out who is responsible for the distortion of the notion of "separation of Church and State." In any case, a fundamentally perverted and rather widespread misinterpretation invokes this "separation" in order to keep God out of a public role in the affairs of men. The extent of this perversion is clearly visible in the recent events that took place in early 1990 in San Diego where individuals arrested for attempting to rescue unborn children from being murdered were prohibited by court order from making any reference to religion, morality, human life, etc. in their defense.

"Keep religion out of politics!" is a slogan frequently invoked by opponents as well as proponents of legalized murder. Hidden behind this slogan, however, is the demand to keep God out of public life. A widespread misinterpretation would reject God's rightful sovereignty over the temporal order and the affairs of men.

45

We have seen the alternative to God's sovereignty: deny that every human individual belongs to God and you must assert that he belongs to the strongest and most powerful. In principle one could argue that we can recognize human rights without invoking God. But in an age where the most basic right — the right to life — is systematically and legally denied, such a position is insufficient. To each individual who claims a right to his life, to each individual who claims the life of another, the same question we have been dealing with must be raised "How did you gain title to the life you claim — your own or the life of another?" The *justification* of such a claim can be grounded only in God, "He gave me my life; He demands an accounting of what I did with it. *Therefore* let none other take it." Without this justification, all human relations must ultimately be reduced to mere power and economics. Thus, each individual would be reduced to considering his own gain and profit as the basis for determining whether to take the life of another or not. And that is precisely the pattern we recognize in the so called "arguments" of the abortionists.

It is God that is the true source of public or civil authority. The "state" has the awesome duty of protecting the rights of every individual who is also a subject of God. And the "state" has the duty and obligation of recognizing its Lord and Sovereign. The "state" must be conscious of *its* title to authority. Failing this it risks becoming tyrannical. It either claims to be its own source of authority, that is, its own absolute, or it claims to derive its authority from the "will of the people." In either case, it exercises its tyranny in the person of those who possess the real power.

It is the same God that stands *above* both Church and State, giving each a different and distinct mission. Each guards and promotes the sovereignty of God but in an essentially different way. Thus, to take an example directly connected to our discussion, the Church, as representative of God in the spiritual realm, is to provide for His honor and the salvation of souls in the confessional, where she absolves the *sinner*, the murderer, the rapist, the thief, the seducer.

The state, on the other hand, has as a part of its mission, also as a representative of God, the sacred and solemn task of protecting and defending the *victims* against the murderer, the rapist, the thief, the seducer.

Each has a distinct, that is, separate mission. The Church can't be expected to take up the sword to defend victims of injustice. And the State can't be expected, or allowed, to absolve the murderer, the rapist or the seducer.

The specifically spiritual mission of the Church, the care for the *inner moral life* of the soul, necessarily precludes the use of force, threats or coercion. She represents God's claims and defends them against the individual himself. To the individual who claims to live only for himself, she says, "*You* belong to God." To the individual who "does his own thing" she urges, "*You* must return to God." And those who hearken, she admonishes, "*You* must repent, renounce your claim to yourself and surrender to God," offering them the means to do so.

Precisely because the submission to the sovereignty of God must be a *free* submission, the use of force, threats or coercion is totally beside the point. Apart from her supernatural means, therefore, the Church can only *teach*. She must try to change the opinions, beliefs or convictions of those who reject the sovereignty of God by proclaiming the truth about God, the truth about man and the truth about the world. It is the truth, not the Church, which demands submission. Hence, it makes no sense to remind or warn the Church that she should not impose "her" morality on others. Morality cannot be imposed. It occurs only in the free response to a moral law.

The state, on the other hand, represents the claims of God over against third parties. To the aggressor who would claim the life of a victim, the state says, "*His* life belongs to him and to God." The fact that the aggressors may not believe in God is totally irrelevant, as is the inner condition of their souls. Their beliefs, opinions and convictions do not matter. The one thing that matters is that their *behavior* threatens to dispossess others of what belongs to the other. The state has the obligation and authority to use whatever force, threat or coercion necessary to prevent such behavior. The mission of the state in this respect is directed to the external sphere of actions and not to the inner sphere of the soul as such. Its task is to defend the *just* claims of each individual to what is his own.

It makes no sense, therefore, to say that legislation against abortion is the legislation of *morality* or the imposition of opinions on others. No, it is the legislation of *justice*, namely the formal protection of rights by the authority and power of the state. The legitimacy of state authority depends on its acceptance of the mission of justice. When it formally abdicates its mission of protecting the most basic right, namely the right to life, it loses legitimacy. It may retain the appearance of legitimacy as it continues to extend the protection of political, religious, and economic rights, indeed, as it creates new rights. But all of this — guaranteed welfare checks, school lunches, retirement, equal opportunity, Medicare, etc. — means nothing if the state does not guarantee the right to life.

The single issue, therefore, centers on the answer to the question "To whom does man belong?"

VII. Abortion:
The Economics of Killing
in the Free Market

It is not at all easy to convince modern man that the public authority of the state is grounded in God's sovereignty. One could argue, as we have done, that if man does not belong to God, he will simply belong to the strongest. We could also show that in such a case he will become the slave of his own passions and desires. But this would hardly advance our dialogue. For the new modern religion is a religion of self-satisfaction and self-realization, dedicated to the filling of the inner need and emptiness of man. At the very heart of this new religion is the ritual of appropriation. Its basic word is "Mine." As the hungry and thirsty man swallows and consumes the external world, making it a part of him, so too, modern man appropriates everything outside of him as something to be consumed and incorporated into himself. This is the position of Marx who spoke of the external world as the inorganic body of man. And this is the very consumerism so unequivocally condemned by Pope John Paul II.

It is imperative that we clearly understand what is involved in this consumerism. When man makes the satisfaction of his own needs the primary and exclusive object of all his striving, two things necessarily follow. First, he will claim as his own, that is, appropriate anything and everything that serves his satisfaction. Second, he *loses possession of himself.* The two are interrelated. Marx saw this. And Christ taught it.

For Marx, capitalism did not allow for the satisfaction of human needs because of *private property*, that is, because individuals claimed things as their own. Marx was not against man's self-centeredness. He simply deplored the fact that it could not be satisfied as long as anyone claimed anything for his own. His solution was to abolish private property. And that which is most private and belongs to man in the fullest sense is his own being, his own freedom. For Marx, then, the abolition of individual freedom, of man's self-possession was the condition for the satisfaction of needs. In other words, Marx and his followers promised satisfaction of all need, that is, paradise on earth or what is also called "quality of life" for a *price*: giving up one's own being. None other than Christ Himself confirmed the truth of Marxist economics! He clearly indicated the *cost* of living for oneself and one's satisfaction: "He who tries to save his life will lose it!"

What an irony of truly historic proportions: even as the communist empire begins to crumble, and the democratic and capitalist countries stir in growing excitement at the prospect of new markets, the wraith of Marx has emigrated from the land of slaves to the West where it finally found the freedom to assume shape and substance! Yes, we have freedom here. A freedom unparalleled in the history of man.

The ghost of Marx was exhausted into impotence by the slaves who had nothing, not even their children, but only their being. External force was not enough to claim this inner being as the price for the promised paradise. Quite simply, considering the price, there was no market for the quality of life offered by Marx. Did the ghost of Marx have to wait a hundred years for the development of the capitalist West to learn that only in a free market would man freely offer his being in order to gain the world? Is it the spirit of Marx that moves Gorbachev to openness, given the realization that the most effective way to realize the goal of Communism is the free market? No abstract, academic questions, these. Who can ignore the price of human dignity paid by many a young man for a copy of the Hungarian edition of Playboy? Who can deny the expanded market in which human life became both commodity and currency with the legalization of abortion in Rumania?

Not a few criticisms have been leveled recently at John Paul II for his alleged socialism and for his alleged failure to understand capitalism and the free market economy. With the above comments I too risk castigation for failing to understand the free market. So I hasten to add that there is nothing wrong with freedom in the market place. I heartily agree with those who say that the government should stay out of the marketplace. But I also insist that it is the task of the government to keep the market from becoming a slave auction. By all means, let everyone have the freedom in building and marketing a mousetrap. But let no man make human life and dignity a commodity in the market place. And let no merchant put an exchange value on man, woman or child. Economics and medicine are *human* activities. Neither supply and demand nor skill in the use of scalpel or curette guarantee their humanity. When human life is bought and sold we no longer have to do with a free market but rather with a slave market. No market can be free and human when human life is bought and sold. The scalpel or curette in the hands of an abortionist is the murder of a human being by butchery and no longer medicine, which by essence and definition is to serve the human.

How often over the years of my involvement in the pro-life cause have I heard the economic factor invoked! So many thousands of dollars to raise each unwanted child to the age of eighteen. And horrors! Most of the burden would fall on taxpayers. The callousness and venality of this approach were so revolting that I failed to see something. Only recently did it become clear to me that it was indeed a question of economics. It was only the answers that differed. The questions were the same on both sides: "How much is a human life worth?" "To whom does human life belong?"

We already saw the answer of Marxist economics. Private ownership of my being is something that has to be given up in exchange for the satisfaction of human needs. And the satisfaction of these needs was the sole end of human existence. Marxist economics, therefore, is doomed to contradiction and nihilism. In the pursuit of self-satisfaction the individual becomes "hooked" and addicted. Satisfaction is purchased at the cost of self-possession: "He who seeks to save his own life will lose it." Ultimately human life is treated as nothing when it is squandered for something less than itself. The philosophy of the abortionist in effect holds that human life is not worth anything without career, health, wealth, education, comfort, etc.

If human life comes to nothing when exchanged for something less than itself, it must be worth everything when it is exchanged for something more than itself: "He who loses his life for my sake will find it!"

Christ too entered into the free market and conferred infinite worth and dignity on human existence by redeeming it with His own life. He reestablished God's sovereignty and kingdom with the primary liturgical word "Thine" spoken on His and our behalf.

VIII. Conclusion:
Rescuing the Innocent
and Redeeming the Sacred

What does this mean for the pro-life movement?
Let us retrace our steps briefly. We have seen the two
radical alternatives: either human life belongs to God or
it belongs to man. The pro-abortionist takes the latter
position. He appropriates human life, both his own and
that of others to use it as payment for something that is
worth less than life itself: career, wealth, health or even
pleasure. From this perspective the state simply becomes
the representative of the interests of those who hold
power. In the "democratic" state, this would be the
interests of the majority, or the interests of that group
which dominates a market formed of various interest
groups. In such a market, the "value" of human life is
determined by the demand for "quality life." And, as any
neophyte in marketing can tell us, progress is a function
of the creation and intensification of needs. At that
point it is inevitable that the consumer loses possession

of himself and becomes consumed by his own need for satisfaction.

In such a market, human life is appropriated and exchanged at will. The government's role is to maintain an unrestricted flow of this human currency, and in the service of the market place, to protect every new need created by the market as a "right."

The atheist is confronted with an existential contradiction, an absurdity. Man is to appropriate himself, to take possession of his being. But in doing so, man loses possession of himself, he becomes an addict to his own needs. In the end he loses the capacity for the very thing that every abortionist uses to justify himself: the capacity to make a *decision*. The overwhelming proliferation of various forms of addiction in our culture gives sufficient evidence to the truth of Christ's words: "He who tries to save his life will lose it."

In the face of such a position dialogue is useless and even counterproductive. The abortionist is not interested in our arguments. In taking the life of innocent victims he invokes sheer power and the satisfaction of his needs. He respects only power even if he doesn't understand it. Hence, confronted with a great enough power that says "We shall stop thee!" the abortionist will in the end be forced to ask "Why?" At that time he will be ready for dialogue. At that time he might be willing to listen to the reasons why he *ought not* take innocent life.

We are obligated in strict justice and in charity to use power to save innocent lives. This obligation devolves on each of us *individually*. It also falls upon *the civil authority*, not as a representative of our collective interests, but rather, as representative of God's interest and His sovereignty.

As we have already seen, human life is *sacred*. It belongs to God by virtue of the fact that He is its *author*. It belongs to man by virtue of the fact that it is a *gift* to us. We are called to take possession of it, but only so that we can give it in return to God and to our neighbor in acts of self-donation and devotion. Thus God's sovereignty over a personal creature is realized in a fuller and more perfect way when that person gives himself, that is, *subjects* himself freely to God. By virtue of the fact that we have a common Sovereign, *we are bound to* protect *others* who belong to the same Lord. Every innocent victim belongs to us the moment he is unjustly attacked. But even more importantly, the helplessness of the innocent binds us: *we* come to *belong to the innocent victims* in a new and unique fashion.

In virtue of the above, God has given us the power to take possession of our beings. He has also given us the power to defend that self-possession in others. But the use of this power is ultimately meaningful and effective only if it is used in imitation of Christ.

It is Christ's Redemption of human life at the price of His own life that gives Him a new and higher title to the ownership of human life. His redemption is the only justifiable instance where human life can become a commodity as well as a currency. Our life was the commodity offered for exchange. His life was the medium of exchange. It was *legitimate* because human life was offered for something higher, namely, divine life. It was *just* because it fulfilled God's demand of His creature, namely, a demand for self-donation and submission which only the Son of God could accomplish. And in both cases it was a *sacrifice*, a giving up of something which was good and which belonged to Him. Hence it was also a supreme evidence of *love*, because God did not simply give us something good, but rather gave Himself up, renounced Himself, as it were, for our sake — first by emptying Himself of His divinity, and then by giving up his humanity with the last drop of blood.

Christ's Redemption, then, is to be the model and the basis for our use of power in rescuing the innocent. This means that we have to give up, to sacrifice something that is our own in exchange for the lives of the innocent. In the secular world, and especially in our Western culture, politics has become an extension of economics: where we are unable or unwilling to pay a price for what we want — and paying a price always involves giving up something that belongs to us — we simply turn to power in order to appropriate what we want. In our secularized culture, the use of political power may mean giving up something of what we *want*, but never of something which we already *have*.

Our *rescue of the innocent* may surely use contemporary power politics and the democratic "process." But it *must also be a redemption*. Individuals in rescue operations have shown their willingness to sacrifice. It is necessary, however, to stress that the sacrifice should not be in vain. By this I mean that it must force the opposition to give up something that it has. The opposition has cheapened human life by exchanging it for career, wealth, health and pleasure. We must raise the price of human life for those who have devalued it. If we raise the price that they must pay even as we show our readiness to sacrifice our own career, health, wealth and pleasure, perhaps they will hesitate and ask us "Why?"

The state derives its legitimate authority from the fact that it represents the Sovereignty of God. It defends in the first place His interest, and not that of individuals or even the collective. Only in the second place does it defend the individuals' rights which are defensible only because man's claim to himself is grounded in his ownership by God. In the third place, it can also defend the interest of various groups or of the majority, but only on the condition that it not violate God's sovereignty or the rights of individuals.

The death penalty exacted by the state is primarily a public vindication of the rights of the Sovereign God to

the life of the innocent victim.   So many of the
arguments against the death penalty recognize implicitly
that it can not be justified if the only function of the state
is the promotion of the interests of its members.   With
the rejection of God's sovereignty it is impossible to
justify the death penalty, even as a deterrent.   But the
death penalty is at the same time a reaffirmation of the
value of human life.   Human life cannot be exchanged as
currency for anything less than itself.   The value of an
innocent human victim must be reaffirmed, even against
the murderer's will.

Until the state reestablishes itself on a legitimate
foundation and exercises its authority as a representative
of God's sovereignty, it must be individuals as such who
respond directly to the call for help by the legitimate use
of power.

As noted, this power depends on the twofold
requirement of sacrificing what is ours and raising the
cost to the abortionist, that is, forcing him to give up
what he claims or already possesses as a price for taking
innocent life.   The recent boycotts of South Africa are a
concrete example.   We must begin by "disinvesting," by
giving up ownership of whatever stands at the periphery
of our being.   We can no longer continue to support or
invest in an economy that caters to extravagant needs
while it sacrifices the lives of the most helpless of the
helpless.   But in disinvesting in a society which protects
abortion corporately and legally, we should not simply

turn what was ours over to the abortionists. That would be mundane economics as usual. Our Lord's exhortation, "He who gives up his life for my sake, will find it" calls for a celestial economics. Whatever we give up we should "keep."

Every dollar saved by giving up a soft drink, a movie, new clothes or new cars should go into the construction of maternity clinics, schools, homes for large families, etc. We need to create a new market for goods and services that will affirm and enhance human dignity rather than commercialize it. The formation of a new, human and therefore alternate economy will surely demand that we give up more than soft drinks, movies, television and clothes. Career and wealth may have to be staked. But here again, they should not simply be given away, but rather reinvested in the service of human dignity and innocence.

The loss of time, freedom, earnings and wealth resulting from the operations rescuing the innocent are noble and heroic and certainly fruitful to the extent that they save lives. I do not counsel discontinuing them. But I do see the need to ground them in a movement so strong and broad that it will produce a seismic shock every time a rescuer is arrested. Surely we want the hackles of the murderer to rise, in fear, not in indignation, every time he hears "Thou shalt not take innocent life . . ." But this can happen only if those dedicated to the defense of the unborn establish base communities that form a new society of service as alternative to our society of consumption.

In the Catholic tradition, the asceticism of self-denial is a liberation of the individual from an attachment to the self which will prevent self-donation to another and to Christ. I am convinced that the present wholesale attack on the unborn innocent calls for an imitation of Christ in His redemption of man. We belong to Christ. We belong to the helpless unborn. Only in devoting ourselves and what is ours to Him and to each of the unborn will we be saved — and they with us.

Christendom College
2101 Shenandoah Shores Road
Front Royal, VA 22630
(703) 636-2900